FRANCIS FRITH'S

COULSDON, CHIPSTEAD AND WOODMANSTERNE

PHOTOGRAPHIC MEMORIES

ROGER PACKHAM is Chairman of the Bourne Society, which is believed to be the largest local history society in England. He has lived in Caterham for over twenty years and has written books on the neighbouring parishes of Coulsdon, Limpsfield, Lingfield and Oxted. He is also co-series editor of the Bourne Society's Village History series, which has so far published eight volumes.

FRANCIS FRITH'S
PHOTOGRAPHIC MEMORIES

COULSDON, CHIPSTEAD AND WOODMANSTERNE

PHOTOGRAPHIC MEMORIES

ROGER PACKHAM

First published in the United Kingdom in 2004 by
Frith Book Company Ltd

Limited Hardback Subscribers Edition Published in 2004
ISBN 1-85937-916-8

Paperback Edition 2004
ISBN 1-85937-917-6

British Library Cataloguing in Publication Data

Francis Frith's Coulsdon, Chipstead and Woodmansterne -
Photographic Memories
Roger Packham

Frith Book Company Ltd
Frith's Barn, Teffont,
Salisbury, Wiltshire SP3 5QP
Tel: +44 (0) 1722 716 376
Email: info@francisfrith.co.uk
www.francisfrith.co.uk

Printed and bound in Great Britain

Front Cover: **COULSDON,** *Brighton Road c1955* C165023t
Frontispiece: **COULSDON,** *Brighton Road 1906* 57075

*The colour-tinting is for illustrative purposes only, and is not
intended to be historically accurate*

CONTENTS

FRANCIS FRITH
VICTORIAN PIONEER

FRANCIS FRITH, founder of the world-famous photographic archive, was a complex and multi-talented man. A devout Quaker and a highly successful Victorian businessman, he was philosophical by nature and pioneering in outlook.

By 1855 he had already established a wholesale grocery business in Liverpool, and sold it for the astonishing sum of £200,000, which is the equivalent today of over £15,000,000. Now a very rich man, he was able to indulge his passion for travel. As a child he had pored over travel books written by early explorers, and his fancy and imagination had been stirred by family holidays to the sublime mountain regions of Wales and Scotland. 'What lands of spirit-stirring and enriching scenes and places!' he had written. He was to return to these scenes of grandeur in later years to 'recapture the thousands of vivid and tender memories', but with a different purpose. Now in his thirties, and captivated by the new science of photography, Frith set out on a series of pioneering journeys up the Nile and to the Near East that occupied him from 1856 until 1860.

INTRIGUE AND EXPLORATION

These far-flung journeys were packed with intrigue and adventure. In his life story, written when he was sixty-three, Frith tells of being held captive by bandits, and of fighting 'an awful midnight battle to the very point of surrender with a deadly pack of hungry, wild dogs'. Wearing flowing Arab costume, Frith arrived at Akaba by camel sixty years before Lawrence of Arabia, where he encountered 'desert princes and rival sheikhs, blazing with jewel-hilted swords'.

He was the first photographer to venture beyond the sixth cataract of the Nile. Africa was still the mysterious 'Dark Continent', and Stanley and Livingstone's historic meeting was a decade into the future. The conditions for picture taking confound belief. He laboured for hours in his wicker dark-room in the sweltering heat of the desert, while the volatile chemicals fizzed dangerously in their trays. Back in London he exhibited his photographs and was 'rapturously cheered' by members of the Royal Society. His reputation as a photographer was made overnight.

VENTURE OF A LIFE-TIME

Characteristically, Frith quickly spotted the opportunity to create a new business as a specialist publisher of photographs. He lived in an era of immense and sometimes violent change.

For the poor in the early part of Victoria's reign work was exhausting and the hours long, and people had precious little free time to enjoy themselves. Most had no transport other than a cart or gig at their disposal, and rarely travelled far beyond the boundaries of their own town or village. However, by the 1870s the railways had threaded their way across the country, and Bank Holidays and half-day Saturdays had been made obligatory by Act of Parliament. All of a sudden the working man and his family were able to enjoy days out and see a little more of the world.

With typical business acumen, Francis Frith foresaw that these new tourists would enjoy having souvenirs to commemorate their days out. In 1860 he married Mary Ann Rosling and set out on a new career: his aim was to photograph every city, town and village in Britain. For the next thirty years he travelled the country by train and by pony and trap, producing fine photographs of seaside resorts and beauty spots that were keenly bought by millions of Victorians. These prints were painstakingly pasted into family albums and pored over during the dark nights of winter, rekindling precious memories of summer excursions.

THE RISE OF FRITH & CO

Frith's studio was soon supplying retail shops all over the country. To meet the demand he gathered about him a small team of photographers, and published the work of independent artist-photographers of the calibre of Roger Fenton and Francis Bedford. In order to gain some understanding of the scale of Frith's business one only has to look at the catalogue issued by Frith & Co in 1886: it runs to some 670 pages, listing not only many thousands of views of the British Isles but also many photographs of most European countries, and China, Japan, the USA and Canada - note the sample page shown on page 9 from the hand-written Frith & Co ledgers recording the pictures. By 1890 Frith had created the greatest specialist photographic publishing company in the world, with over 2,000 sales outlets - more than the combined number that Boots and WH Smith have today! The picture on the next page shows the Frith & Co display board at Ingleton in the Yorkshire Dales (left of window). Beautifully constructed with a mahogany frame and gilt inserts, it could display up to a dozen local scenes.

POSTCARD BONANZA

The ever-popular holiday postcard we know today took many years to develop. In 1870 the Post Office issued the first plain cards, with a pre-printed stamp on one face. In 1894 they allowed other publishers' cards to be sent through the mail with an attached adhesive halfpenny stamp. Demand grew rapidly, and in 1895 a new size of postcard was permitted called the court card, but there was little room for illustration. In 1899, a year after Frith's death, a new card measuring 5.5 x 3.5 inches became the standard format, but it was not until 1902 that the divided back came into being, so that the address and message could be on one face and a full-size illustration on the other. Frith & Co were in the vanguard of postcard development: Frith's sons Eustace and Cyril continued their father's monumental task, expanding the number of views offered to the public and recording more and more places in Britain, as the coasts and countryside were opened up to mass travel.

Francis Frith had died in 1898 at his villa in Cannes, his great project still growing. The archive he created continued in business for another seventy years. By 1970 it contained over a third of a million pictures showing 7,000 British towns and villages.

FRANCIS FRITH'S LEGACY

Frith's legacy to us today is of immense significance and value, for the magnificent archive of evocative photographs he created provides a unique record of change in the cities, towns and villages throughout Britain over a century and more. Frith and his fellow studio photographers revisited locations many times down the years to update their views, compiling for us an enthralling and colourful pageant of British life and character.

We are fortunate that Frith was dedicated to recording the minutiae of everyday life. For it is this sheer wealth of visual data, the painstaking chronicle of changes in dress, transport, street layouts, buildings, housing, engineering and landscape that captivates us so much today. His remarkable images offer us a powerful link with the past and with the lives of our ancestors.

THE VALUE OF THE ARCHIVE TODAY

Computers have now made it possible for Frith's many thousands of images to be accessed almost instantly. Frith's images are increasingly used as visual resources, by social historians, by researchers into genealogy and ancestry, by architects and town planners, and by teachers involved in local history projects.

In addition, the archive offers every one of us an opportunity to examine the places where we and our families have lived and worked down the years. Highly successful in Frith's own era, the archive is now, a century and more on, entering a new phase of popularity. Historians consider the Francis Frith Collection to be of prime national importance. It is the only archive of its kind remaining in private ownership. Francis Frith's archive is now housed in an historic timber barn in the beautiful village of Teffont in Wiltshire. Its founder would not recognize the archive office as it is today. In place of the many thousands of dusty boxes containing glass plate negatives and an all-pervading odour of photographic chemicals, there are now ranks of computer screens. He would be amazed to watch his images travelling round the world at unimaginable speeds through internet lines.

The archive's future is both bright and exciting. Francis Frith, with his unshakeable belief in making photographs available to the greatest number of people, would undoubtedly approve of what is being done today with his lifetime's work. His photographs depicting our shared past are now bringing pleasure and enlightenment to millions around the world a century and more after his death.

COULSDON, CHIPSTEAD AND WOODMANSTERNE

AN INTRODUCTION

THE THREE parishes of Coulsdon, Chipstead and Woodmansterne have their origins as hilltop settlements on the Surrey hills, once remote from London but now on the outskirts of Greater London. Domesday Book records them in AD1086, although there was no mention of a church at Chipstead. Fragments of the Saxon church at Coulsdon survive in the old part of St John's, Old Coulsdon.

The villages retained their traditional way of life, largely involving agriculture based on scattered farms, until the late 19th century. In each parish it was the railway that had the effect not only of increasing the population but of moving the village centre from the old established hilltops down to the valleys. In 1921 the populations of Chipstead and Woodmansterne were still only 992 and 667 respectively, whilst in Coulsdon, expanded by a large community at Cane Hill Hospital, it was 5823.

The process of moving the traditional centres was first evident at Coulsdon. It had long been a farming community centred on the present day Old Coulsdon. Taunton Farm, Bradmore Farm, Tollers Farm and others together with windmills, a workhouse and a school were presided over by

the church and a lord of the manor who, from 1782 to 1921, was a member of the Byron family. In the valley generally known as Smitham Bottom an early railway had appeared in 1805 before the Brighton line was constructed in 1841. Despite some road transport including stagecoaches, the road through Smitham Bottom, now the A23, remained uninhabited apart from the Red Lion, Stoats Nest Farm and Hooley House until 1883, when Cane Hill Hospital was opened. From that date cottages, shops, stations, schools, pumping stations, libraries and new roads have appeared with some rapidity and the area has claimed the name of the old parish, Coulsdon. The area around St John's Church was intensively developed in the 1930s.

In Chipstead the old part of the village has retained much of its character and the absence of street lighting and buses has preserved a rural atmosphere. Some of Chipstead's farms, unlike Coulsdon's, are still worked. The railway was late arriving at Chipstead and it was not until 1897 that Chipstead Station was opened although it is in the parish of Woodmansterne. The development along Chipstead Valley towards Coulsdon largely took place in the 1930s.

Woodmansterne Station, situated in Coulsdon, did not arrive until 1932 and, although some distance from the old village, it was an important factor in the development of new roads off Rectory Lane as well as the profusion of roads in west Coulsdon.

The photographic record importantly shows the villages at different stages of their expansion and repays careful study in understanding the way they have evolved. This record can be usefully supplemented by several other sources including official records, local newspapers and personal reminiscences. Of the latter W G Gardner, station-master at Coulsdon South from 1891, recorded in 1916 the growth of the parish from a hamlet to an urban district: 'Red Lion Green was a Green in every particular in those days. Very few houses were in existence excepting the old thatched cottages facing the Chipstead Valley Road. ...Cornfields were seen where the Fairdene Estate now rises whilst High Street, Coulsdon [Brighton Road] did not exist. Truly a revolution in the short space of a quarter of a century.'

In 1962 Mrs C Nicholls, born in 1872, recalled walking to St John's School, Bradmore Green from Hooley: 'We used to walk up to the Star [near Star Lane], turn left over the railway bridge, through lanes and across Farthing Down, then more lanes. We also had this walk when I and my sisters attended St John's Church for Sunday School. Later I remember going to Sunday School in a tin hut situated where the Comrades Club now stands... We children used to wait by the side of the main road for the London and Brighton stage coaches, The Age, The Comet and Old Times, to pass, when we called out "throw out your mouldy coppers." One gentleman thought he was tossing down a halfpenny but it turned out to be a golden sovereign...Mother walked to Croydon to shop pushing a perambulator with wooden wheels and iron tyres and I often went too...There were only about six shops in what is now called Coulsdon but which was then known as Smitham Bottom. They were all in old cottages converted to shops. The nearest station was Caterham Junction [Purley]. When I first knew Chipstead Valley, the road was only a narrow lane, with rough flint surface and no lighting. The only traffic was an occasional farm wagon or flock of sheep...The fields where Richmond and Alexander Roads are now always used to have

COULSDON, *The Recreation Ground c1955* C165050

11

lots of poppies and looked very pretty.'

In 1970 Marjorie Harvey recalled Chipstead as she remembered it in 1910: 'There were at that time three main estates in Chipstead - Longshaw, Shabden Park and Elmore. Shabden Park was owned by Lord and Lady Marshall and their activities were great in the village: they employed game-keepers, gardeners, coachmen, footmen and many staff in the House. They were good employers and the annual Flower Show was always held in a field near the House. It was a day's outing to go to that show, for there were swing-boats, merry-go-rounds, side-shows of all descriptions and a local brass band which played during the afternoon, besides all the marquees with the exhibits. Longshaw was owned by Mr Bravington, a director of the famous jewellery company. Mr Bravington loved horses and he possessed twenty thoroughbred hunters which my father had to look after. He used to hunt around Chipstead and the meets sometimes started from the stable yard at Longshaw with all the ladies and gentlemen in their colourful attire. Mr Cheeseman owned Elmore and every Christmas the children of the village had a huge Christmas tree in the Peter Aubertin Hall where the Sunday School prizes were presented…There were only two shops in the village then, the grocery store and little old hardware shop owned by the Barnards. There were carriers' carts which used to come up from Coulsdon bringing bread, fish and some groceries, but if one wanted to shop in Coulsdon, it was a real red-letter day as you had to walk to Chipstead Station and get a steam train. There were no houses from Woodmansterne Water Works until you got right into Coulsdon and of course no

station at Woodmansterne. With the coming of the First World War everything went haywire. The Government commandeered all the beautiful horses that Mr Bravington had, for shipment to France to pull the guns. My father said that Mr Bravington cried when he saw his horses go - they never came back!'

In 1945, Miss Wedd looked back to the 1880s in Woodmansterne: 'Derby Day was a most important event in the neighbourhood of Woodmansterne. The railway to Tattenham Corner had not been opened and every kind of conveyance, coach, carriage, cart and wheelbarrow, or rather donkey shay, came through the village. The village children would run perilously close along the sides of the road, throwing little bunches of flowers into the passing vehicles. There must have been many narrow escapes from being run over as they collected the pennies tossed to them for the flowers, and the hedges of the lane from The Oaks were white with dust for days afterwards. Before and after the races the children had the amusement of seeing parties of gypsies on their way to and from the course…' Miss Wedd remembered skating on the small pond in the Manor House stable paddock or on the larger pond at Martin's (Clockhouse) and the wonderful opportunities for collecting wild flowers which included martagon, or turks' cap lilies, bee or fly orchid and twayblade, very rare wild flowers. She also enjoyed the view from Carshalton Road, which included the Crystal Palace with its two great flanking towers, which crowned the horizon and was a lovely landmark for many miles around. Miss Wedd also wrote of the cottages in the village being of wood and some falling into decay, in which lived gardeners and other men employed in the houses of the gentry. On the left of the Manor House there was a large muddy pond, which had once formed the main water supply of the village. Its close proximity to the house, though screened from it by the magnificent horse chestnut trees, must have been something of a nuisance for the greater part of it was filled in and a concrete bottom put to what was left. Miss Wedd remembered the building of a very ugly, wooden, black-tarred house, facing down the village street and at right angles to the Court Haw gates in which a shop was opened and which later became the first post office in Woodmansterne. Previously the only shop had been a tiny one at the end of Court Haw Terrace.

The three villages face the 21st century with some confidence. Although Coulsdon, at the southern end of a densely populated London Borough, has all the problems associated with such - traffic congestion, affordable housing, infilling, petty crime - its old hilltop settlement at Old Coulsdon is largely unchanged since the development of the 1930s. Its open spaces continue to delight visitors and residents in great numbers. At Chipstead, despite the closure of the village school and shops in the old village, the old area supports a thriving community in a rural setting. Woodmansterne's ancient buildings in The Street were swept away in the 20th century but the neighbourhood around St Peter's Church is still vibrant and the inter-war development towards Chipstead Valley has become a desirable residential area.

The geographical position of Chipstead and Woodmansterne means that residents do not necessarily gravitate towards Coulsdon for social and commercial requirements. Banstead provides many of these services and is included in this photographic record along with neighbouring Kingswood and Burgh Heath. Other local villages featured are Kenley, historically within Coulsdon parish, Warlingham and Whyteleafe.

WARLINGHAM, *'Ye Olde Whyte Lion' 1903* 50546

COULSDON

COULSDON, *St John's Church and Lychgate 1906*
57079

St John's Church has been at the heart of the parish since Saxon times although the main core of the present building dates from 1260. The side chapel with a chimney stack on the right of the photograph was demolished to make way for the enlargement, completed in 1958. The flint wall on the right is now obscured by a neighbouring hedge and the monkey puzzle tree has vanished.

COULSDON
Brighton Road
c1955 C165030

The southern approach to Coulsdon is seen on a lovely summer's day. There is no need for traffic lights at the Lion Green Road junction and a well maintained seating area greets the passers by. The trees on the right screen the sidings of Coulsdon North Station, the line of which is shortly to be used for the new Coulsdon by-pass.

COULSDON, *Brighton Road c1906* 57075

A young girl with a pram stands outside the gates and vanished lodge house of Cane Hill Hospital, built in 1883.
The building in the centre, obscured by a tree, was at this time Coppard's Temperance Hotel, a favourite haunt of cyclists.
New houses are appearing in the distance on Smitham Downs.

▼ **COULSDON,** *Brighton Road c1960* C165056

Few traffic controls are in evidence at the southern end of the shopping area in about 1960. Cars queuing to come out of Lion Green Road by Thomas Ebbutt's undertaker's business anticipate the need for traffic lights at this junction of two busy A roads. The railings of Cane Hill Hospital are on the left.

► **COULSDON**
Brighton Road c1955
C165023

The grassy area enclosed by a chain link fence disappeared with increasing traffic but in the mid 1950s traffic was light and the three cyclists feel unthreatened. Beyond is a garage run by Leon A Davis and the white, detached building beyond the line of Victorian cottages is the Comrades Club. St Andrew's Church dominates the residential area to the west of Brighton Road.

◄ **COULSDON**
Brighton Road
c1965 C165066

A Victorian terrace was demolished to make way for the commanding Tesco store in the early 1960s, but after several changes the building presently houses the Kabada restaurant, a snooker hall and the Thai Venue. On the right, Mr Grover's business of garden ornaments and fencing has now been replaced by lines of second-hand cars on the corner of Station Approach.

► **COULSDON**
Brighton Road
c1965 C165067

The Red Lion public house, the Water Works and Coulsdon Library on the east side of Brighton Road contrast in style and date with the Victorian terraced houses and shops opposite. The Water Works building has been replaced by Sentinel House and the Red Lion survives in 2004, boarded up and awaiting demolition.

COULSDON
High Street c1955
C165038

In the mid 1950s car owners could park outside the shops and cyclists could leave their bicycles outside the library. The shops visible include Pink Bros (radio engineers), World's Stores, Phyllis (ladies' fashions), Croll (newsagent's), The Pattern Shop, Doe (butcher's) and, at the junction of Chipstead Valley Road, National Provincial Bank and Woolworth's.

COULSDON, *The Public Library c1955* C165012

The Library and adjacent buildings on the left are of more recent date than those on the right because there was a regular problem with flooding on this side of the road, caused by the local Bourne stream. The Library was opened in May 1936, following the purchase of the land from the Southern Railway.

COULSDON
The Red Lion Hotel
1906 57073

The Red Lion can be traced back to 1680 and stood alone until the arrival of the railways and Cane Hill Hospital. This building, with its splendid mansard roof, was demolished in 1927 to be replaced by the present mock Tudor public house now awaiting demolition. Note the brewery sign for Watney, Coombe, Reid & Co, the ornamental lamps and weighing machine.

COULSDON, *Brighton Road c1955* C165042

Although fifty years have passed the centre of Coulsdon is easily recognisable, although the forthcoming replacement of the Red Lion will dramatically alter appearances. Looking towards the Smitham railway bridge, the United Dairies' building has been replaced by Waitrose. The zebra crossing has disappeared as has the police box, and the four red telephone boxes have been replaced by a single kiosk.

COULSDON
Brighton Road c1955
C165031

The evolution of local shops can be clearly traced in this mid-1950s photograph. The traditional baker's and butcher's (Hearn) are housed in the Victorian terrace to the left followed by the taller, later buildings which include a house agent, Freeman, Hardy & Willis, and Boots. A butcher, baker, shoe shop and estate agent are still found in this parade.

▲ **COULSDON,** *Brighton Road c1955* C165073

The card shop and Susan Starr are now occupied by Abbey and Martyn James (butcher's), whilst Bond & Sherwill and Stead & Simpson maintain the presence of an estate agent and a shoe shop. Boots has moved a few shops further on. On the right hand side the four gables now mark four long-standing businesses, those of Downside Pharmacy, the Coulsdon Fish Bar, Jeff Dee and Pandora News.

▲ **COULSDON,** *Brighton Road c1965* C165072

The corner of Windermere Road and Brighton Road marks the point where this photograph was taken. The empty shop on the left is now occupied by Doble's motor cycles. The Seeboard shop on the corner of The Avenue is currently Threshers off-licence, whilst on the right the bookshop now houses a video shop. Next to Westminster Bank, Marsh's cards and artists' shop arrived in 1925.

▲**COULSDON,** *Brighton Road c1955* C165024

A train on the Smitham railway bridge adds interest to this photograph of the northern end of Brighton Road shopping area. Older readers will remember the United Dairies shop on the corner of Malcolm Road, since replaced by Waitrose. The tall building on the right is Lloyds Bank. This part of Brighton Road is due to benefit from the construction of the Coulsdon by-pass, commenced in 2004. It is many years since advertising was displayed on the railway bridge.

► **COULSDON**
Chipstead Valley Road c1965
C165071

The white-fronted building on the left housed Burridge's furniture shop when this photograph was taken in the mid 1960s. Today Coulsdon Home Hardware has moved here from Brighton Road and opposite, Newman's and Midvale Snack Bar have now become Pulcinella cafe and Singapore Orchid. Mr Woods' jeweller's has survived and the shops protected by the striped blind also include Kenyon's (estate agents), a copy shop and a shoe repairer.

◄ **COULSDON**
Chipstead Valley Road c1955 C165032

There are no parking restrictions in this busy view looking towards the junction with Brighton Road. A snack bar and Coulsdon Fish Bar suggest that the fast food phenomenon is not new to the area. Gosling's wool shop and children's wear is now a wedding services shop. The shops on the left lead towards Woolworth's and were built as private homes subsequently converted to shop use.

▲ **COULSDON,** *Chipstead Valley Road c1955* C165034

The road leading to Chipstead Valley is dominated by Edwardian terraced houses on the right. There are three churches visible which are St Aidan's, in the distance, the original Coulsdon Baptist Church (an iron hall built in 1936) and the former Elim Pentecostal Church with its Italian marble pillars. The Victorian St Dunstan's Cottages, left, were built for staff at Cane Hill Hospital.

◄ **COULSDON**
St Aidan's Church
c1955 C165046

This Roman Catholic Church has assumed an entirely different appearance since this photograph was taken. In 1964 it was discovered that the foundations were defective and a complete re-building, with foundations taken down to solid chalk, was implemented. The present church dates from 1966. St Aidan's has its origins in a hall in Woodcote Grove Road but moved to the above site in 1931.

COULSDON
*Woodcote Grove
Road c1955* C165033

The gabled row of houses leads towards a railway bridge with St Andrew's Church beyond. The houses were built in the early 1900s when the road was part of Smitham Bottom Road and now preside over a continual flow of traffic as part of the A237. The trees on the right hide the playground and buildings of Smitham School which has since relocated to Portnalls Road.

COULSDON, *St Andrew's Church c1965* C165069

Woodmansterne Road leads towards the crossroads with Woodcote Grove Road and The Avenue overlooked by St Andrew's Church. The Lord Bishop of Southwark cut the first sod on 30 October 1913 and a year later the church was consecrated by the Bishop of Kingston. It remained incomplete until 1964 and commands the area with an illuminated cross on the tower that shines out over the valley.

COULSDON
The Avenue c1955
C165041

A pleasing mixture of Edwardian houses lines the northern side of The Avenue on its descent to Brighton Road and the shops near the Smitham railway bridge. The left-hand turn down the hill is The Grove, another development from the early 1900s. The semi-detached houses on the left, now Nos 22 and 20, were originally named Netherton and Alleyne and the neighbouring house was Inglenook.

COULSDON, *Downs Road c1955* C165027

The houses on the right are Nos 18 and 20 Downs Road, formerly called Fanfare Road when built on the northern slopes of Farthing Down. Beyond the motorcar the road turns sharply to meet the busy Brighton Road south of Coulsdon. The road to the left climbs to the crest of Farthing Down and was only constructed after much local opposition.

27

▶ **COULSDON**
*The Sign Post,
Farthing Down
c1965* C165052

The signpost makes a central focal point on the flat-topped ridge looking towards the solid tower of Cane Hill Hospital on the skyline. The 121 acres of Farthing Down have in recent years seen the introduction of a small herd of cattle to graze the coarser grasses. The area here is known as The Folly and nearby a millennium cairn has appeared.

◀ **COULSDON**
*Farthing Down
c1955* C165035

A beautifully composed photograph captures the western slopes of Farthing Down looking south towards the tower of Netherne Hospital, surrounded by wild flowers, mature trees and footpaths. The remains of Cuthraed, a Saxon king, were discovered nearby and it is considered that his name is contained in the first element of the place-name of Coulsdon.

▲ **COULSDON,** *The View from Farthing Down c1955* C165054

A fine panoramic view of east Coulsdon shows the extent of the development in the late 1920s and 1930s in Marlpit Lane, Bradmore Way and neighbouring roads. Prior to this development, only Marlpit Farm would have been visible from the slopes of Farthing Down. A narrow hedge-lined Marlpit Lane linking Coulsdon to Old Coulsdon survived until its widening in 1928.

◄**COULSDON**
*The View from the
Downs c1955* C165026

The backs of the houses in Chaldon Way near the turning with Bradmore Way are viewed here from the footpath along the line of magnificent yews on the eastern slopes of Farthing Down. The poplars by Purley CGS for Girls can be seen on the left skyline.

◄**COULSDON**
Marlpit Lane 1906
57076

The narrow hedge-lined lane with unspoiled views over the Brighton Road valley remained until the late 1920s when the lane was widened and houses rapidly appeared. The five-bar gate marks the present entrance to Hillside Road whilst opposite is to-day's Stoneyfield Road. The lane was a great favourite with cyclists in the early 1900s.

The View from the Downs c1960 C165025

The back views of houses in Marlpit Lane are shown in a view looking towards the Memorial Ground and the chalk pit. The latter was operated for many years by Hall & Co's Limeworks and there is evidence of smelting from the industrial building. The chalk pit has now given way to Ullswater Business Park and houses in Nineacres Way.

◄ COULSDON
Purley County Grammar School c1955 C165019

It is regrettable that these fine school buildings in Stoneyfield Road, opened in 1939, were sold in 1992 and the land is now covered by houses in Rossetti Gardens and neighbouring roads. At the end of the war there were 520 girls on the registers, many of whom will remember the headmistress, Miss J C Simpson, who presided until 1962.

COULSDON
The Common c1955
C165037

The two semi-detached houses are viewed from Coulsdon Common owned and managed by the Corporation of London. The two houses are in Fox Lane and the nearer was formerly the Calabar Cafe, still fondly recalled by local residents. Some new houses have since appeared on the corner of Coulsdon Road and the older house on the left has been demolished.

COULSDON, *The Common c1955* C165044

Fox Lane runs behind the trees, drinking fountain and seats on its way to Old Fox Close and the Fox public house. On the opposite side of the hedge the Coulsdon Workhouse, built in 1805 and now a private house, survives to the present day.

COULSDON, *The Recreation Ground c1955* C165050

The Memorial Ground in Marlpit Lane was opened in 1921 in memory of the men who fell in the First World War, the land being donated by Edmund Byron of Coulsdon Court. From 1947 to 1973 the ground was used by East Coulsdon Cricket Club, formed from the local residents' association. The cafe on the right originally had a thatched roof.

► **COULSDON**
*The Recreation Ground
and the Bowling Green
c1955* C165014

The well maintained greens
of the Memorial Ground
provide an ideal setting for
some serious ends of bowls
with good seating for
spectators. Alongside is a
miniature golf course as well
as facilities for cricket and
tennis. Old Coulsdon
Bowling Club in Coulsdon
Road, formed in 1936, also
provides excellent greens.

◄ **COULSDON**
The Recreation Ground
c1955 C165029

A lone figure walks downhill from the war memorial at the Memorial Ground in Marlpit Lane. The memorial was dedicated on 16 April 1921 and contains the names of 76 local men who died in the Great War. The trees by the entrance to the ground, left, have been replaced by an expanded parking area.

CHIPSTEAD

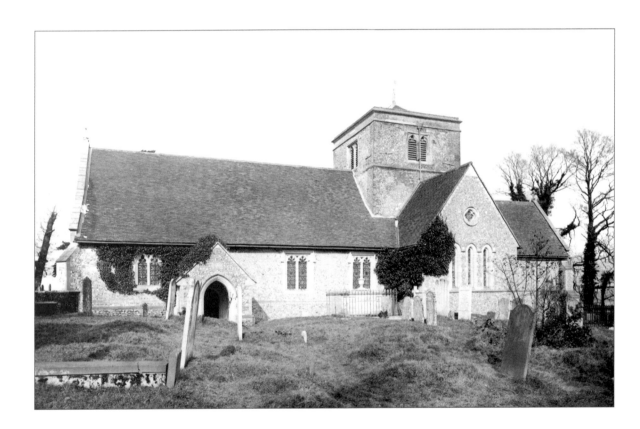

CHIPSTEAD, *The Church 1886* 18940

The south side of St Margaret's Church is seen looking across the churchyard from Church Lane. The earliest parts of the church date from the 12th century, there is no mention of a church here appearing in Domesday Book. The railings around Sir James Little's tomb to the right of the porch have now disappeared. The gravestone in the foreground to the right marks poor Mary Ann Wood, who died on 18 June 1797, aged 14 months.

CHIPSTEAD
The Church c1960
C484301

The war memorial on Church Green was designed by Hugh Scott-Willey and records the 44 men from the parish who lost their lives during two world wars. The lychgate conceals the fine west doorway to St Margaret's.

CHIPSTEAD, *Fair Dene School c1960* C484049

The school moved to the above buildings from Coulsdon in 1948, when two head teachers acquired Pirbright from Sir Walter and Lady Moberly. Pirbright, in Hogscross Lane, is an ancient manor and is mentioned in Domesday Book as being held by Chertsey Abbey. The brick structure on the right is part of the 17th century farmhouse with the remainder being Victorian extensions. The school left the premises in 1984.

CHIPSTEAD
Ruffetts Cottages
c1955 C484002

Ruffetts Cottages, High Road, on the right probably date from the early 18th century and at one time belonged to the Shabden Estate. When the village policeman Joe England retired from duty he moved here and converted the cottages to one dwelling. The more modern house next door is Nightingale Cottage, built for Nurse Smith in 1923.

CHIPSTEAD, *The Cottage c1960* C484053

A wealth of timbers, tiles, gables, chimney-stacks and a thatched gateway make another attractive High Road house north of Ruffetts Cottages. It is now obscured by trees and hedges. J A Garle built the house c1900, and its former residents include Stanley Holloway and cartoonist Tom Webster. Some remnants from Newgate Prison were used in the construction.

CHIPSTEAD, *Hogs Cross c1955* C484024

The signpost does not notify the traveller that Hogscross Lane is in the foreground with High Road running left to right, and White Hill runs downhill towards Mugswell and Kingswood. The fence on the right marks the extent of Shabden Park and its disappearance now gives a much more open appearance across attractive downland.

▼ **CHIPSTEAD,** *The Cross Roads c1960* C484034

The beautiful mature trees make an attractive setting in high summer along High Road at its junction with White Hill, extreme left, and Hogscross Lane. The fencing on the left has now been replaced by a wire fence and the sign post, still on its grassy triangle, has been modernised and now includes directions to the M25.

► **CHIPSTEAD**
Shabden Park Hospital c1955 C484052

Shabden Park was used as a hospital from 1936-76 following Lord Marshall's death. It is described by Nairn and Pevsner as 'Very Victorian-French Renaissance' and dates from c1870 though the estate is mentioned in the assize rolls of 1253. In 1910 Sir Horace Marshall bought it and on occasions he entertained the future King Edward VIII and George VI to shooting parties. The south front shown here is now divided by a hedge.

◄ CHIPSTEAD
Shabden Cottages
c1955 C484005

The scout hut, agricultural vehicle and long forgotten signboard are features of the left-hand side of High Road looking towards Elmore Pond. On the opposite side of the road the sturdy Shabden Cottages, built in 1871, make an attractive row of former estate workers' cottages. Beyond, a timber structure can be seen in the front garden of No 1. It was for many years the village post office.

► CHIPSTEAD
Elmore Cottages
c1955 C484006

Elmore Cottages still command the High Road opposite the village pond and crossroads but have been extended on the south side where the fence on the flint wall has been removed. The cottages originally formed part of an estate comprising the large house of Elmore and its lodge house. The original Elmore was demolished c1925 by Alexander Dods.

CHIPSTEAD
The Pond c1960
C484040

Elmore Pond always provides a pleasing feature for travellers along High Road and now has a perimeter footpath. Beyond the trees to the right is the large open space of The Meads, the home of Chipstead Rugby Club. The Meads were given to Banstead UDC by the Stoddart and Wates families in 1964.

CHIPSTEAD, *The White Hart c1955* C484031

The White Hart has been a public house since at least 1775 when it was a smallholding with five or six acres of farmland. Bounded by Hazelwood Lane and High Road, the property appears in title deeds going back to the 17th century. Licensees since the war include Frank Adams, Mr Rogers, Arthur and Lilian Lane and Mike Austin.

CHIPSTEAD
High Road c1960
C484032

Gatefield Cottages shown here on the eastern side of High Road were built in the early 1900s by Frank Goad, owner of The Lodge in Hazelwood Lane. The cottages take their name from Gatefield, which is now part of The Meads. Beyond the vehicle is the entrance to Starrock Lane by Vincent's Green.

CHIPSTEAD, *Starrock Lane c1960* C484027

This delightful sunken lane is one of Chipstead's secrets, linking Vincent's Green with Coulsdon Lane. The flint wall on the left, now dismantled, is probably marking the entrance to Keepers. In the 1950s, Seretse Khama of Basutoland spent his exile in Starrock Lane.

CHIPSTEAD
High Road c1965
C484045

Frank Butcher's newsagent and tobacconist shop at the north end of High Road has a well stocked window but alas has now been demolished, and the other shops have closed. The shop on the right, built in 1885, is now a private house called Old Chipstead Stores. Merrythought Cottage is the protruding building on the left.

▶ **CHIPSTEAD**
The Valley c1955
C484020

The sinuous valley of the Tattenham Corner branch-line threads its way through the contours at the foot of Banstead Downs on the right. In the centre can be seen the viaduct taking the railway over Outwood Lane on its way to Kingswood. The line was opened in 1897, partly as a speculation by Sir Cosmo Bonsor.

◄ CHIPSTEAD
Outwood Lane c1960
C484030

The Corner Shop and Station Parade Post Office still provides an invaluable service to residents and passers-by, but an extension has been built on to the end wall for Saab who also trade from the garage premises shown here. George Jones commenced running The Corner Shop in 1966 with his wife, Pat.

CHIPSTEAD
Station Parade c1955
C484022

The off-licence on the
corner of Lackford Road
and Station Parade no
longer sells Watney's ales,
and currently remains
empty with a chartered
architect's name by the
door. Apart from The
Corner Shop at the far end
of the parade, trading here
has changed its nature with
the second and third shops
in the foreground now used
by Palmer's chartered
accountants and RJS
heating and plumbing.

CHIPSTEAD
The Mid-Day Sun
c1955 C484035

Although the name of The Mid-Day Sun has not completely disappeared, the more prominent signs for this 1930s public house are now for The Hungry Horse. The original name recalls a Derby winner. The garage was for many years Cronk's, but it has been re-built as Prospect Wells House for a spring water company. The pub's gable front is now weather-boarded.

WOODMANSTERNE

WOODMANSTERNE, *St Peter's Church c1955*
W507002

The visitor to St Peter's now has a very different view of the north side of the church than when this photograph was taken. Four large windows have been inserted in the extension of 1961 and the porch has been moved outwards. The chimney has vanished but two clock faces appear on the tower and gable. A church here was mentioned in Domesday Book, and was rebuilt in 1876-7.

WOODMANSTERNE
The Green c1960
W507029

A stately cedar tree dominates the Green on the corner of Carshalton Road, Rectory Lane and Woodmansterne Street. Sadly it now lies fallen awaiting the saw. In the centre is the lychgate to St Peter's but the trees to the right have been removed, to provide a better view of the church.

WOODMANSTERNE, *Carshalton Road c1960* W507031

The photograph was taken opposite the Scouts Headquarters looking along the B278 towards Oaks Park. The three houses each contain three dwellings and are numbered 40 to 56 from right to left. The modern development of Merrymeet has been built behind the houses.

WOODMANSTERNE
The Street c1955
W507010

Two girls seem unimpressed by a boy playing leapfrog on a summer's day fifty years ago. Opposite, E Wynne's shop has now lost its black and white appearance with rendering and is currently Mystique Hair Design. Looking towards Chipstead Way the other shops are now a golf shop, photographer's and the post office with the old style telephone box replaced by a modern kiosk.

▲ WOODMANSTERNE
The Woodman c1955 W507028

A hundred years ago when Mr Flinders was the licensee the Woodman was not open on Sundays, but trade has increased to the extent that seats and tables now line the forecourt. The turret has now been tiled to cover up the distinctive diamond and the loss of the mature tree with the inn sign is to be regretted.

► **DETAIL FROM** W507028

WOODMANSTERNE, *The Street c1900* W507301

Looking west towards Court Haw, a horse and carriage wait patiently outside the little single-storey post office built on to the side of a large house, all now swept away. In the foreground is an itinerant traveller, proudly standing by his barrel organ, partly covered by canvas and mounted on a handcart. There appears to be a lamp alongside.

◄ **WOODMANSTERNE**
The Original Oak,
Chipstead Way c1955
W507027

The old village of
Woodmansterne is behind
the photographer, who is
looking towards the
Chipstead valley via the
switchback road of
Chipstead Way. The latter
was built between the
wars and contrasts with
Rectory Lane, the
alternative approach to
the old village, which still
retains its rural qualities.
The semi-detached house
on the left is numbered 49
and 51.

WOODMANSTERNE
Rectory Lane c1955
W507016

A parade of local shops photographed from the junction with Pine Walk is dominated by T H Shepherd (tobacconist and stationer). Today the corner shop is Surrey News & Mini Market and, although there is still a hair salon next door, the adjacent shops have changed character to include two financial advisers, a security shop, floor shop, a vet and a Chinese restaurant. Beyond the shops is the pumping station built in 1907.

WOODMANSTERNE
Pine Walk c1955
W507017

Chipstead Way runs immediately behind the photographer's position and Upper Pines is the turning on the left-hand side beyond Nos 44 and 42 Pine Walk. The hill in the background with a hedge on its crest remains an attractive focal point from this 1930s development. At the end of the road is Woodmansterne Baptist Church, which moved here from Chipstead Valley Road, Coulsdon.

WOODMANSTERNE
Manor Way c1955
W507001

A pre-war motorcar of much character is parked outside 63 Manor Way on the corner of Chipstead Way, whilst a modern delivery van runs downhill towards Rectory Lane. In the distance there are still fields separating the parishes of Woodmansterne and Coulsdon.

WOODMANSTERNE
Rectory Lane c1955
W507003

Fifty years ago there was far less traffic at the southern end of Rectory Lane but otherwise the scene is remarkably unchanged, with the inter-war housing contrasting with the hedge and embankment on the opposite side. In the centre, the prominent single gable houses Nos 63 and 65.

WOODMANSTERNE, *Rectory Lane c1960* W507033

Only a modern lamp-post detracts from the rural tranquility of Rectory Lane on its way to the old village. The disappearance of the distinctive fence on the left makes the exact location hard to determine but it is likely that the photograph was taken just south of The Old School House on the left and Eastlands Farm House on the right.

WOODMANSTERNE
Banstead Downs
c1955 W507019

Holly Lane and Park Road converge on Park Downs, with the stable block of Park Farm in the centre with its distinctive clock tower. The trees and bushes to the left of the picture have been cleared away to create a large car park.

WOODMANSTERNE, *Chipstead Valley c1955* W507022

The slopes below Banstead Wood make a fine vantage point above Outwood Lane meandering on its way towards Kingswood. Left of centre is the sprawling old house called Stagbury, a late 18th-century house demolished in the 1970s. Within the parish of Woodmansterne, it was home to the Walpole family, which has an impressive tombstone in St Margaret's, Chipstead.

THE SURROUNDING AREA

KINGSWOOD, *The Village c1955* K156006

Fifty years ago the main A217 road through Lower Kingswood had not yet been widened. Beyond the bus stop the cluster of petrol pumps has been replaced by a BP garage slightly lower down the hill, and the garage on the right has been re-built as GVC (Vans Direct). Beyond the clock the Victorian gable has a date of 1884.

KINGSWOOD, *The Parish Church c1955* K156038

This is an unusual view of St Andrew's Church, taken from the graveyard looking west towards the main road. The church was consecrated in 1852 by the Bishop of Winchester and a lunch was held in the grounds of Kingswood Warren in 2002 to celebrate the 150th anniversary. The gravestone on the extreme left relates to the Costain family and Sir Albert's name was added when he died in 1987.

▶ **KINGSWOOD**
Station Approach
c1965 K156039

The Station Hotel, later the Pigeon Pair and now the Kingswood Arms, now has a profusion of flowers along its frontage as well as tables and chairs outside. The hotel was built when the railway arrived at Kingswood in 1897, and it still commands this part of Waterhouse Lane at its junction with Bonsor Drive and St Monica's Road.

◄ KINGSWOOD
Waterhouse Lane c1965
K156047

Mr Chappell's newsagent's and post office is fondly recalled by local residents but is now a Londis store. Surprisingly, Hocken's chemist's shop next door is now Hocken's Audio Visual Ltd. The garage is now occupied by Mitsubishi Kingswood and beyond is the Kyber Tandoori.

KINGSWOOD
The Station c1965
K156043

Kingswood Station was the original terminus on the branch line from Purley when it was opened in 1897. The attractive design of the station was influenced by the demands of Sir Cosmo Bonsor of Kingswood Warren, for whom the line was constructed. There had been an earlier canopy but reports of this supporting a tea terrace have been doubted.

▼ **BURGH HEATH,** *The Sugar Bowl c1955* B723020

The Sugar Bowl with its colourful decorations is seen from the opposite side of a narrow-looking Brighton Road. The restaurant was later Il Pirata but the building has been demolished and replaced by the present travel lodge and inn known as Heathside.

► **BURGH HEATH**
Il Pirata c1960 B723034

Il Pirata, with its elaborate model ship to attract customers, is viewed here on the A217 south of the village. It enjoyed a reputation as a restaurant and for dinner-dances, but has been rebuilt as Heathside with an accommodation block.

◀ **BURGH HEATH**
Brighton Road
c1955 B723005

The parade of shops at the junction of Reigate Road and Brighton Road has an unfamiliar appearance without traffic lights and the extensive Shell Garage. The single-storey builder's shop on the right has given way to a substantial building currently housing Burgh Heath Tandoori.

▶ **BURGH HEATH**
The Parade c1965
B723026

The service road alongside The Parade has now been incorporated into the busy A217, looking south towards today's traffic lights at the junction with Reigate Road. The old house at the end of the parade housing Holmes & Co butcher's (established 1824) was demolished for road widening. A laundrette has replaced the cycle shop and Pressley Wilkins is now shared by a television repair shop and a hairdresser's.

BURGH HEATH
The Galleon c1955
B723014

Reigate Road presents an
unfamiliar appearance,
looking east towards
Brighton Road, where the
Galleon swimming pool has
given way to a busy petrol
station. Apart from the
rooftops of Burgh Heath
Parade all these buildings
have been demolished, as
has the tree in the centre.
There is no doubt which
shop the owner of the car
on the right has just visited.

▼ **BURGH HEATH,** *Reigate Road c1965* B723028

Only the Burgh Heath Parade and the petrol station are recognisable today in this view from The Green, Reigate Road. The latest demolition has been the Surrey Yeoman public house on the left, which has been replaced by Yeoman Court.

▶ **BANSTEAD**
The Church 1903 50300

All Saints' Church is seen from the footpath from Avenue Road, with High Street behind the trees on the right. It dates from the 13th century although a church was recorded here in the time of Domesday. Over the years there have been many additions and alterations, notably in the 1860s and in 1899.

◄ **BANSTEAD**
High Street c1955
B391013

Fifty years ago the high street had assumed its present busy appearance, and it is seen here from opposite All Saints' Church. Collinson's shop on the left is now Oscar's hairdresser's, with a Scope charity shop next door.

► **BANSTEAD**
High Street c1955
B391006

The parade of shops on the left are currently occupied by Thomas Cook, Abbey, a hairstylist and a photographic shop, whilst Boots is in the adjacent block. On the opposite side of the road a parade of shops has replaced the undertaker's and surrounding houses. The village school beyond has given way to Waitrose.

BANSTEAD
The Village 1903 50302

This delightful collection of village buildings graced the eastern end of High Street until demolished by a flying bomb in 1944. The Woolpack, right, was re-built further back from the road. Church records show that parish business was conducted here in 1715. The wall of Well House is in the background.

BANSTEAD, *The Old Well 1903* 50304

The 18th-century wellhead covering the winding gear to a 300ft well survives at the junction of Park Road and Woodmansterne Lane. Well House, behind, was built in about 1650, bought by Sir Daniel Lambert in 1739 and demolished in 1963. The village relied on water from wells until the arrival of piped water.

KENLEY, *The View from the Railway Station 1903* 50536

Carriage building and slaughtering are in evidence in Station Road on the eastern side of Kenley Station, along with some neat Victorian houses. Trees and shrubs on Riddlesdown are not nearly so dense as they have since become. The chimney on the right belonged to Kenley Water Works.

KENLEY, *From Riddlesdown 1903* 50531

The recently built houses in the area known as Roke are photographed from the slopes of Riddlesdown. The house and shops on the line of Godstone Road, now replaced by Secom House, are just south of the turning for Little Roke Road. The hills and fields in the distance have mainly been built over.

KENLEY
From the Oaks 1903
50533

One of the ancient oaks that gave its name to the area known as Roke provides shelter for two local children. Behind them is the gate marking the crossing of the railway, since replaced by a footbridge and on the other side of the hedge are Oak Cottages on the edge of Kenley Cricket Club, but now demolished.

KENLEY, *Godstone Road 1903* 50535

The Kenley Hotel on the corner of Hayes Lane was built soon after Kenley Station arrived in 1856. On the opposite corner is Yateley House, the home for many years of the local doctors. The name of the house is recalled by a nearby block of flats. All Saints' Church can be seen in the distance.

KENLEY, *Riddlesdown Tea Gardens 1903* 50542

Although Gardner's Tea Rooms were closed in 1934 after 38 years, the house survives complete with historic blue plaque.
In addition to the tea-rooms shown here on the left there were amusements including donkey rides, a miniature railway,
swingboats, and Ike, a monkey brought back from the Boer War.

WHYTELEAFE
The Tabernacle and Coffee Tavern 1907
57467

This extensive building on the corner of Godstone Road and Station Road was demolished in 1966 and the site is now a car park for local shoppers and commuters. The tabernacle was built in 1892 by John Newberry, who died in 1928 leaving the property to the Salvation Army who relinquished it in 1960.

▼ **WHYTELEAFE,** *Station Road c1955* W93003

A tree-lined Station Road draws the eye towards Upper Warlingham Station, which arrived in Whyteleafe in 1884. Older residents will recall the clothing shop and its predecessor Allan's furniture shop, as well as the Co-op and Stevenson & Rush. The latter is now occupied by a fish and chip shop on the corner of Godstone Road.

▶ **WHYTELEAFE**
The Square c1950
W93008

In common with many villages, Whyteleafe's local shops have reduced in numbers and those on the left have been demolished. Next door, a Blue Star garage, previously Surrey County Garage from the early 1900s, expanded to become a car showroom but was demolished in 1986.

▼ **WHYTELEAFE,** *The Square c1955* W93006

The ribbon development along the line of Godstone Road is well illustrated here, looking north towards Riddlesdown chalkpit. The traffic bollards at the junction of Whyteleafe Hill and Hillbury Road have been replaced by a roundabout. The parade of shops, right, has been demolished but those beyond have reverted to private houses.

► **WHYTELEAFE**
Godstone Road
c1955 W93001

Traffic restrictions and the roundabout by the Whyteleafe Tavern are still many years away, but the post office remains at 217 Godstone Road on the right. It moved here in the mid-1930s, when it was run by Spencer and Arrundale. Mr Trowse, bootmaker and repairer, traded next door from the 1930s but after the war it became Chandler's cycle shop.

◄ **WARLINGHAM**
Ye Olde Whyte Lion
1903 50546

The White Lion is a listed Grade II building dating from the 17th century, with a southern wing added about a hundred years ago. Recent alterations have provoked considerable local opposition. A smartly dressed party, possibly celebrating a christening, assemble beneath a sign showing the landlord's name whilst in the background the name of Lee is shown on The Horseshoe. The Working Men's Club, opened in 1902, is on the other side of the road.

◄ WARLINGHAM
The Village 1903
50543

Warlingham Green with a line of saplings is overlooked by Mr Ringer's Warlingham & Chelsham Supply Stores. The turning for Glebe Road is by the double-fronted house in the centre, and the National Provincial Bank was later built on the opposite corner. On the opposite side of the road a workman is putting up a fence later to be painted with a sign for Warlingham Tea Gardens.

◄ WARLINGHAM
The School 1904 51276

Warlingham School is seen from Westhall Road one hundred years ago. It was opened in 1874 with 75 pupils, some of whom came from Whyteleafe. Following its closure in 1982 the school stood empty for five years apart from occupation by some squatters. The site was redeveloped and Redvers Court was completed in May 1989.

WARLINGHAM
The Old Forge 1907
59240

Blanchard's forge and Forge Cottage with neighbouring dovecote make an attractive setting in Farleigh Road. Beyond is a glimpse of a house called The Meadows, demolished in 1986. The site of the forge and the agricultural machinery is now occupied by a modern house. The oldest part of Forge Cottage dates from the 17th century.

WARLINGHAM, *The Harrow Inn 1904* 51279

The Croydon brewery of Nalder & Collyer sold its ales at a rural-looking Harrow Inn 100 years ago. The property was originally called Aynescombes and included Home Field and Pond Field, although a large roadside pond nearby no longer exists. The inn has undergone extensive improvement and enlargement in recent years.

INDEX

NAMES OF SUBSCRIBERS

The following people have kindly supported this book by subscribing to copies before publication

In memory of Mr & Mrs Anderson

Mr G Bellenger & Mrs J L Bellenger of Coulsdon

Mr R P & Mrs K M Boolaky, Coulsdon

The Brind Family, Coulsdon

Richard Carter on his 80th Birthday 2004

Dorothy Church, Coulsdon

Coulsdon & Purley Advertiser

Eve Gordon & Freckles, Fairdene Road

The Guilfoyle Family, Old Coulsdon

Martin Hambrey, Coulsdon

Ian Harmer & Wendy Bailey, Coulsdon

D T Hathaway and C Westgate, Chipstead

J Hill

The Huggett Family, Coulsdon

Charles King

Roger W King

John Lindley & Family

Jeff, Sheila, Helen & Jo Lovell, Coulsdon

Pat McEachen, Coulsdon

In memory of Richard Mantell, Coulsdon

The Munday Family, Woodmansterne

John P Murray

Peter Norman

Mr M J Page

Maureen Pattenden, Coulsdon

'For the good times' - The Peacocks, Coulsdon

J Peters

Derek & Beryl Peters, Coulsdon

Mr & Mrs Redman

The Reed Family, Old Coulsdon

Michael F Rhodes, Coulsdon

Tim Sanders

Paul Sandford, Purley

Brian R Smith, Old Coulsdon

Bob, Margaret, Robert & Katie Smith

P R Smithers

Mr & Mrs P J Smith

Sheila & Andrew Swaine, Coulsdon

John Sweetman

Den Taylor, Woodplace Lane, Cousldon

The Taylor Family

Mr & Mrs R J Tew, Coulsdon

Peter & Susie Thompson

Fred Turner & Diane Mills, Cousldon

Mr & Mrs C J & A J Webb

Paula Welch

The Williams Family

Mr S & Mrs P Williams

Leonard Wilson & Patricia Wilson, 2004

Chris & Vicki Wood and Family, Coulsdon

FRITH PRODUCTS & SERVICES

Francis Frith would doubtless be pleased to know that the pioneering publishing venture he started in 1860 still continues today. Over a hundred and forty years later, The Francis Frith Collection continues in the same innovative tradition and is now one of the foremost publishers of vintage photographs in the world. Some of the current activities include:

Interior Decoration

Today Frith's photographs can be seen framed and as giant wall murals in thousands of pubs, restaurants, hotels, banks, retail stores and other public buildings throughout the country. In every case they enhance the unique local atmosphere of the places they depict and provide reminders of gentler days in an increasingly busy and frenetic world.

Product Promotions

Frith products are used by many major companies to promote the sales of their own products or to reinforce their own history and heritage. Frith promotions have been used by Hovis bread, Courage beers, Scots Porage Oats, Colman's mustard, Cadbury's foods, Mellow Birds coffee, Dunhill pipe tobacco, Guinness, and Bulmer's Cider.

Genealogy and Family History

As the interest in family history and roots grows world-wide, more and more people are turning to Frith's photographs of Great Britain for images of the towns, villages and streets where their ancestors lived; and, of course, photographs of the churches and chapels where their ancestors were christened, married and buried are an essential part of every genealogy tree and family album.

Frith Products

All Frith photographs are available Framed or just as Mounted Prints and Posters (size 23 x 16 inches). These may be ordered from the address below. From time to time other products - Address Books, Calendars, Table Mats, etc - are available.

The Internet

Already fifty thousand Frith photographs can be viewed and purchased on the internet through the Frith websites and a myriad of partner sites.

For more detailed information on Frith companies and products, look at these sites:

www.francisfrith.co.uk
www.francisfrith.com
(for North American visitors)

See the complete list of Frith Books at:

www.francisfrith.co.uk

This web site is regularly updated with the latest list of publications from the Frith Book Company. If you wish to buy books relating to another part of the country that your local bookshop does not stock, you may purchase on-line.

For further information, trade, or author enquiries please contact us at the address below:
The Francis Frith Collection, Frith's Barn, Teffont, Salisbury, Wiltshire, England SP3 5QP.
Tel: +44 (0)1722 716 376 Fax: +44 (0)1722 716 881 Email: sales@francisfrith.co.uk

See Frith books on the internet at www.francisfrith.co.uk

FREE PRINT OF YOUR CHOICE

Mounted Print
Overall size 14 x 11 inches (355 x 280mm)

Choose any Frith photograph in this book.
Simply complete the Voucher opposite and return it with your remittance for £2.25 (to cover postage and handling) and we will print the photograph of your choice in SEPIA (size 11 x 8 inches) and supply it in a cream mount with a burgundy rule line (overall size 14 x 11 inches).
Please note: **photographs with a reference number starting with a "Z" are not Frith photographs and cannot be supplied under this offer.**
Offer valid for delivery to UK addresses only.

PLUS: Order additional Mounted Prints at HALF PRICE - £7.49 each (normally £14.99)
If you would like to order more Frith prints from this book, possibly as gifts for friends and family, you can buy them at half price (with no additional postage and handling costs).

PLUS: Have your Mounted Prints framed
For an extra £14.95 per print you can have your mounted print(s) framed in an elegant polished wood and gilt moulding, overall size 16 x 13 inches (no additional postage and handling required).

IMPORTANT!

These special prices are only available if you use this form to order . You must use the ORIGINAL VOUCHER on this page (no copies permitted). We can only despatch to one address. This offer cannot be combined with any other offer.

Send completed Voucher form to:
The Francis Frith Collection, Frith's Barn, Teffont, Salisbury, Wiltshire SP3 5QP

CHOOSE A PHOTOGRAPH FROM THIS BOOK

Voucher for **FREE** and Reduced Price Frith Prints

Please do not photocopy this voucher. Only the original is valid, so please fill it in, cut it out and return it to us with your order.

Picture ref no	Page no	Qty	Mounted @ £7.49	Framed + £14.95	Total Cost
		1	Free of charge*	£	£
			£7.49	£	£
			£7.49	£	£
			£7.49	£	£
			£7.49	£	£
			£7.49	£	£

Please allow 28 days for delivery

* Post & handling (UK) £2.25

Total Order Cost £

Title of this book . . . .

I enclose a cheque/postal order for £ . . . .
made payable to 'The Francis Frith Collection'

OR please debit my Mastercard / Visa / Switch (Maestro) /Amex card
(credit cards please on all overseas orders), details below

Card Number

Issue No (Switch only)   Valid from (Amex/Switch)

Expires   Signature

Name Mr/Mrs/Ms . . . .
Address . . . .
. . . .
. . . .
. . . . Postcode . . . .
Daytime Tel No . . . .
Email . . . .

Valid to 31/12/07

Would you like to find out more about Francis Frith?

We have recently recruited some entertaining speakers who are happy to visit local groups, clubs and societies to give an illustrated talk documenting Frith's travels and photographs. If you are a member of such a group and are interested in hosting a presentation, we would love to hear from you.

Our speakers bring with them a small selection of our local town and county books, together with sample prints. They are happy to take orders. A small proportion of the order value is donated to the group who have hosted the presentation. The talks are therefore an excellent way of fundraising for small groups and societies.

Can you help us with information about any of the Frith photographs in this book?

We are gradually compiling an historical record for each of the photographs in the Frith archive. It is always fascinating to find out the names of the people shown in the pictures, as well as insights into the shops, buildings and other features depicted.

If you recognize anyone in the photographs in this book, or if you have information not already included in the author's caption, do let us know. We would love to hear from you, and will try to publish it in future books or articles.

Our production team

Frith books are produced by a small dedicated team at offices in the converted Grade II listed 18th-century barn at Teffont near Salisbury, illustrated above. Most have worked with the Frith Collection for many years. All have in common one quality: they have a passion for the Frith Collection. The team is constantly expanding, but currently includes:

Paul Baron, Phillip Brennan, Jason Buck, John Buck, Ruth Butler, Heather Crisp, David Davies, Louis du Mont, Isobel Hall, Gareth Harris, Lucy Hart, Julian Hight, Peter Horne, James Kinnear, Karen Kinnear, Tina Leary, Stuart Login, David Marsh, Lesley-Ann Millard, Sue Molloy, Glenda Morgan, Wayne Morgan, Sarah Roberts, Kate Rotondetto, Dean Scource, Eliza Sackett, Terence Sackett, Sandra Sampson, Adrian Sanders, Sandra Sanger, Jan Scrivens, Julia Skinner, David Smith, Miles Smith, Lewis Taylor, Shelley Tolcher, Lorraine Tuck, Amanita Wainwright and Ricky Williams.

Free Print - see overleaf